Misunderstood Silence:
A Guide to Effective Communication with Your Mate

By: Jeffrey & Chanel Nash

CANNONPUBLISHING

Misunderstood Silence:
A Guide to Effective Communication with Your Mate

By: Jeffrey & Chanel Nash

CANNONPUBLISHING

Published by: Cannon Publishing.
Cannon Publishing P.O. Box 1298
Greenville, NC 27835
Author owns complete rights to this book and may be contacted in regards to distribution.

Printed in the United States of America

First Printing, 2015
ISBN-13:978-1515161509
ISBN-10:1515161501

Ordering Information:

Quantity Sales. Special discounts are available on quantity purchases by corporations, associations, and others via www.iamchanelnash.com.

Book Cover Design: Bobby Barnhill
Editorial & Services: Cannon Publishing
Formatting Services: Marsena Cook

DEDICATION & THANKS

We would first like to dedicate this book to God, because without him none of this would be possible. To our daughter Gabrielle we love you, and everything we do is for you. To our parents both natural and spiritual we thank you for being our backbone at our darkest hour. Bishop Edward Nash, Willie Nash, Tasha Williams, Apostle Keith Curry & Pastor Keisha Curry. To our family and friends we thank you for the continuous support.

CONTENTS

FOREWORD

I would like to first thank my spiritual son and daughter, Jeffery and Chanel Nash for the privilege of writing their foreword in regards to their very first book in which you are now holding. Being a married man myself to my first love and sweetheart, Kisha Curry for twenty-four years, we literally watched, helped, and guided this wonderful couple through some of the most challenging times in their marriage. While many are writing books from what they have studied or went to college and earned a degree regarding a particular topic of interest, this dynamic couple has written a book based upon their experiences which include their ups and downs, ins and outs along with their triumphs and failures. Therefore, by reading this book you are gaining a glimpse of their now successful marriage which is clear on sharing that marriage is not based on a fantasy. But real marriage is hard work but worth everything each couple has to put into it. The authors, whom I am very proud of cover an array of topics from dealing with infidelity and how they bounced back to becoming one in their marriage in which many are still struggling to do today. My advice to you is for you to sit back, sip on some coffee, grab a few donuts along with your spouse and get ready to learn how to restore or further develop in your marriage from these two great authors whom I love dearly. May the Lord bless you dearly as well as your covenant relationship with one another.

Dr. Keith K. Curry Th.D.DD.D.

INTRODUCTION

From the outside looking in we had it all together. We both had well-paying jobs, nice cars and were financially stable and not to mention young. We would take amazing photos that people swoon over. They would often tell us that they want a relationship like ours not knowing that we were living in hell. From the outside looking in we were living "the dream." We didn't want for anything. We had money to do what we wanted. We bought each other expensive gifts. We put on a show for the world, but we were actually living a double life. We had no clue what we had gotten ourselves into. Our picture was painted so well that even we were fooled by it.

After one year of marriage we hit rock bottom. There was so much chaos that we saw no way out of it, but to get a divorce. How does the picture perfect couple end up at the bottom? How does a wife who seems so dedicated and faithful end up committing infidelity? How does a husband who seems to be doing everything right be so far off? The answer is the same for them all; lack of communication. It seems so simple but yet it is so hard to execute.

My husband and I began to realize that from the beginning we had been talking *at* each other rather than *to* each other. Both of us were talking but neither of us was truly listening. There was never any real understanding of what communication really was on both of our ends. We had no guide, no book or manual before we said our vows. Little did we know that we would spend the next two days on our Apostle's sofa. What we learned in those two days saved our marriage.

The only reason people talk is to get something that they cannot immediately have. Whether it is to gain advice, an object, food, something to drink, sympathy, help and anything else you may need. If you didn't need it from someone other than yourself then you would have no reason to talk at all. This applies to relationships as well. Sadly enough most relationships are in need of restoration but don't know it because they refuse to talk and confront the issues within their relationship..

Most couples aren't having the necessary discussions that will grant longevity in their relationships. People do not realize that the solution to their problems are actually simple. Why do we find communication to be a complex method to incorporate in our relationships? Truth is, there are a lot of people who are not comfortable with talking. We are not referring to the conversations where you partly tell the truth about your feelings.

But more so in regards to the conversations where you both are vulnerable, and a hundred percent open and honest with one another.

These conversations involve transparency; a willingness to step outside of yourself for the other person is a must. You aren't alone in the confusion of what communication is. Most couples if not all have faced communication issues. That's what brings us here right now. To help others see that even if you hit rock bottom you can still bounce back and restore all that appeared to be lost. We had an amazing support system, and we encourage you to do the same. We would not be where we are if it wasn't for the foundation we created with God. We always had God in our corner, but we forgot about him and lost our way. He was just waiting for us to give our marriage back to him. If you make God the center of your relationship instead people you can't go wrong. We had our spiritual parents who kept us grounded. They refused to tell us what we wanted to hear, but they told us what we needed to hear. They would not allow us to take the easy way out, but yet they made us confront our issues and truly hear what the other person had to say. Our parents remained unbiased and encouraged us to make it work. We owe everything to them. In order to make any real progression you must first ask yourselves, *'Are we having the necessary conversations? Are they effective? Are we executing what we are discussing? Are we being consistent in doing better? Are we being open minded? Are we both talking and listening? Are we putting our feelings to the side to get to the root of the problems? Are we willing to compromise? Are we willing to sacrifice?'* There are so many questions we have to ask ourselves regarding our relationships?

The most common thing couples fail to see eye to eye on is expectations, the past, money, sex, friends, family, dreams and goals. There are more but for us these are the ones we hear about the most. We want this book to serve as a reminder as well as a helpful guide on how to overcome any issues you may be experiencing in your relationships and to remind you that you are not alone. We too have experienced things that we thought we would never recover from. As humans we all experience different things but the core issues tend to relate back to a familiar source especially in relationships: lack of communication. The answer to fix all your relationship problems believe it or not, is effective communication. You must learn how to not only talk, but listen as well. Learn how to take criticism, and remember that you are not the only person within this relationship. You may think your communication is just fine, but if there are subjects that are off limits or you try to avoid like the plague there is an issue. It may not seem like a big deal right now, but I can almost guarantee you that if you don't fix it now it will only get worse with time. You'll wake up one day and realize you both are on the brink of walking away. One of you if not the both of you will be wondering how did you all get to this point. One of you may even say "I didn't know it was that bad." Truth is you didn't know because you were not listening when the other person was talking.

CHAPTER 1
Both Sides of the Story

HERS:

The first mistake I made in this relationship was thinking that my husband could replace my father. I put the world on his shoulders and expected him to fix all of the damage. Truth is I had to fix myself. As a child I always felt abandoned and misunderstood. That eventually molded me into a promiscuous young woman searching for love in all the wrong places. It had me believing that I could find true love by freely giving up sex. I never realized that I had already set my husband up for failure. He couldn't fix what he didn't know was broken. He didn't understand just how bad off mentally I really was. He couldn't know because I didn't know.

The second mistake I made was not being completely forward about what I had been through. I didn't give him the opportunity to decide whether he wanted to deal with my baggage or not. I made the decision for him. By the time he saw my true colors he had already invested years. Our issues didn't happen overnight. They started the moment we met. I blame myself for a lot it because I was so busy trying to be perfect. I wanted everyone to believe that I was strong and unbothered. I was really broken, hurt, used and misunderstood. I had no one to talk to. For one I was ashamed, and secondly I didn't think anyone would understand.

I can remember plenty of days wanting to end my own life because life was just that unbearable for me. I didn't think that anyone would truly love me. I knew that all those guys only wanted to have sex with me, but I was just that desperate to have someone even if only for the moment. I wanted so badly to be married. I wanted that family that I never had. Though that's what I wanted I wasn't prepared for it. You may think that I'm making excuses for my infidelity, but I'm simply sharing my story. I was damaged goods, and the only person that was truly capable of helping me heal was God not my husband. We come from two different worlds. He never had a chance of truly helping me heal. I came from a single parent home. My mom had been married and divorced three times. I had no real view of a happy family. My husband on the other hand came from a household with both parents there. They all had the same mother and father, and we all had different fathers. His father was a Bishop and mine was a ghost. He could never really understand even if I told him. He would have never understood no matter how many tears I cried.

Our first year of dating I went off to join the Marine Corps. That alone changed who I was as well. I thought I could run away from my past, but my past found me. My father walked back into my life after 18 years, and one of my molesters apologized to me. I thought things would be different after that, but little did I know heartache would meet me again. Two years into our relationship we found ourselves at the justice of peace saying, "I do." Truthfully we weren't ready. We had no clue what we were getting ourselves into. Six months later we had a big wedding only to fight during most of our honeymoon. We ignored all of the red flags. Despite how bad it was our love was real, and that's what we had to hold onto.

I thought being married would fix all of my problems, but it didn't. The more I ignored my issues the worse they got. I was needy and I craved for attention. My husband had gotten into the routine of working and providing. I was working and going to school full time. I would leave the house at 4 a.m. for work and not return until 11 p.m. from school. We were spending anytime together. If felt like we were more roommates than husband and wife. I was craving attention from my husband and I wasn't getting it. That wasn't his fault, because I never told him I was lacking attention in the first place. I felt like he should have known, but he couldn't read my mind. I never opened my mouth to say how I truly felt. I assumed he knew. I eventually found myself playing with fire and entertaining another man.
I had it all figured out. I was only going to flirt with him nothing more. It couldn't be that harmful. I knew better, and I still played with the fire. I believed that I could control myself.

The more I played the worse it got. I found myself blaming my husband for nothing just to justify why I was doing what I was doing. Eventually I ended up in a hotel with man pretending like nothing would happen. That day I went against my vows. I shattered the trust of my husband. Though he didn't know at the time I betrayed him in the worst way. Not once but twice.

I can remember the pain on my husband's face as he questioned me about what I had done. It was like someone sucked the life out of me. I had finally gotten burned by the fire I had been playing with. Not only had I hurt my husband, but my spiritual and natural parents were so disappointed in me. Heck I was disappointed in me too. Not the fact that I had gotten caught, but the fact that I had sabotaged my own happy ending. I just knew that my husband was leaving me. We went straight to our Apostle's house. All I could do was cry for my husband. It was at that moment I realized how truly messed up I was. Our Apostle was hard on us both, but it was needed. For the first time we really communicated with one another. It was painful to hear, but it saved us. People think I'm crazy when I say this situation saved our marriage. I honestly don't believe we would still be together had we not had that conversation that day. We learned things about each other that we never knew. My husband may see it differently, but this is what it did for me.

Our spiritual parents gave so much advice that we never would have thought of. We took those principals and modified them to our marriage. Though our trust may never be the same, our marriage is better for it. We never dreamed we would get to this place of peace and happiness. I'm not saying it cured us from never having an argument. We still have our moments of disagreements, but now we don't have to worry about if we will be divorced at the end. We are now prepared for the fight. I had to learn that I too deserve happiness, and I don't have to test our relationship to know that what we have is real. I no longer have to play Russian roulette with our marriage. We are open about emotions, and we no longer allow things to build until it explodes. We are here to prevent people from going through what we went through, because all we had to do was talk instead of assume. I assumed that he knew what I was feeling and didn't care, and he assumed that everything was okay. We were both wrong. We are at a point now that even if everything is okay we talk to make sure that we are on the same page.

HIS:

I can remember that day like it was yesterday. I was driving my wife to Wilmington, North Carolina to take a test for the postal services job she just applied for. We joked and laughed all the way there; I felt as though we were in a good place. Little did I know my life would be changed forever on that day.

My wife was inside taking her test and I sat in the car listening to music and on Facebook. My wife's cell phone begins to vibrate. She left the phone in the car because it was not allowed in the building while testing. I picked up her phone to see why it was vibrating; it was an email. I thought nothing of it at the moment. Then I began to go through her text messages and what I read and saw completely shattered my heart. My wife had been sleeping with another man. My entire world flipped upside down in that moment. I begin to rack my brain as to why, when, how did this happen? I didn't want to believe that this was true. I wanted it to be a joke or a mistake. I couldn't believe that the woman I gave my all to would betray me in such a way. This pain that I was feeling was indescribable. I was hurt beyond what words could explain.

 While all this was happening my wife was still inside taking her test. I thought I should leave her in another city 60 miles away from where we were living without a phone or anyway of getting back home. Then a few moments later she walked out of the building and got into the car. I immediately threw her phone on the floor of the car. I began to question her on the messages and what I had seen in her phone. She kept saying, "Let's just go home." I would not leave the parking lot. Then I began to head home then something told me to call my Apostle. I told him that it was urgent and we needed to see him. I immediately drove to his house. My wife and I sat on opposite sides of the sofa and Apostle sat in front of us. We begin to talk about what happened. It was hard to discuss our issues in open forum and be transparent. It was difficult to hear that I played a part in the infidelity as well.

   I was in denial thinking that I was doing everything I needed to do for my wife. It was painful hearing her say how she felt alone. I want to sit and say that I had no clue, but our problems didn't just come out of the blue. We had ignored the signs for so long. We were barley seeing each other. We barely had sex or communicated, but I never thought it was that bad. There's no excuse for what she did, but we both had a hand in our failure.

The tools and advice that we learned those two days saved our marriage. We learned how to communicate with each other and be open but still respectful to one another. We learned how to immediately talk about issues when they happen rather than letting the frustration build. Apostle helped us reestablish order in our marriage. After sitting on his couch for hours and crying and letting all the pain and frustration out we came to a conclusion that neither one of us were perfect in this marriage. We both needed to fix our communication issues.

The transformation did not take place overnight but in those moments that we were on the couch we became closer than we had ever been before. Yes it was hard, there were moments that I had relapsed and I would think about what had happened and I would say that this is it, I cannot do this anymore. There were times that it would play in my mind over and over again. I would always remember my vows and realize that I am not perfect. We all make mistakes. My wife and I have been to hell and back but it has made us who we are. I can honestly say if it was not for the infidelity we probably would not have made it this far. It took something to the magnitude of infidelity to knock us out of the fantasy we had put ourselves in.

CHAPTER 2
What Do You Want?

When we first meet people whom we are considering being in a relationship with, we evaluate them based upon certain things: their age, hobbies, profession: things of that nature. It's not that asking questions is wrong, but the key to building effective and purposeful relationships is asking the right questions. It is understandable that when you are on a first date that you don't go in too deep into whom the person really is. You will typically ask these basic questions if you don't already know the answers. Where do you work? Are you religious? If so, what's your denomination and where do you attend church? Do you have any children? Have you ever been married? How old are you? When is your birthday? We get that, but when you realize that what you two have going on is getting serious your line of questioning must change along with the evolvement of the process. .A common mistake most couples make is they don't ask those deep questions that are critical to building their foundation. For example, did you grow up in single parent household? How is your credit? Do you want children? If they already have children, do they want more children? How do you feel about marriage? What are your expectations of this relationship? What is your opinion on disciplining children? Do you believe in spankings or time out. These questions are so critical to a relationship.

We made this very mistake of not asking the right questions. Who knows if we would have remained together had we asked these questions. We could have avoided so much drama and chaos within our marriage had we only discussed who we were and what we wanted.

Have you ever gotten upset with your partner over something they have done that you expected them *not* to do? Has your partner ever gotten upset with you about something you've done that you didn't think would offend them? If this has happened on numerous occasions don't worry we've been there as well, but just know you need to work on your communication. This happens because couples fail to talk about their expectations. It is so vital that you discuss these matters sooner than later. Discussing your expectations may save you from wasting years of your life. You may even discover that you don't really like that person at all. Time is essential and once it's gone you can't get it back.

Have you ever witnessed a relationship where the couple has been together for years and are finally engaged, only for the guy to say he doesn't want kids? Have you ever seen couples fight over what denomination their kids will follow? Have you ever witnessed a man complain that his wife isn't submissive? These are perfect examples of why there should be an early discussion on expectations. Like we stated before this is where you build your foundation. Take a moment and really think about this.. Is it okay to get upset with your partner over something they had no idea would offend you and perhaps vice versa? A person doesn't know if they haven't been informed. You can't assume that they should know better. An old cliché is a closed mouth doesn't get fed. If you expect for your partner to do something you must be willing to express your concern or desire via conversation with them..

You may think that we are asking you to lower your expectations, but that is far from the point we are trying to make. Your expectations are yours to have, and there is nothing that anyone can do about that. You like what you like and that is completely okay. What you cannot do is assume that someone is going to be willing to go along with your expectations. This is why you must have this conversation with your mate. You have to give your partner the choice of whether or not your expectations are something they willing to sign up for. You cannot make the choice for them. One of the greatest mistakes people make is assuming that their partner will go along with all of their demands or even their desires for that matter. A relationship is all about give and take. You can't just throw out demands without being willing to compromise even a little.

You need to ask those hard questions at the beginning. Do you want kids? If so, how many? What religion do you practice? Do you see marriage in your future? What are your goals or dreams? What is your credit score? Are you a spender or saver? When is the last time you were tested for any STDs? Have you ever been sexually active? Have you ever been married? How is your relationship with your parents? These are all questions that should be discussed and then some. There is no limit on what should be asked when you are considering having this person be a part of your life. This allows you to determine if you two are on one accord which can lead you down the path to a healthy marriage. Don't wait until you say "I do" to have this conversation only to end up in divorce court a week later.

We've discussed what negatives can occur so let's now focus on how to fix it. When thinking of expectations there are no right or wrong answers. What you may expect may not be what your partner expects. No two people are the same. The only way to know what your partner desires from you is to sit down and ask them!. Have a serious discussion on what it is that you need from that person. Don't be afraid to question their expectations. If you need to know why they want something done a certain way ask them to explain. There is nothing worse than having someone upset with you for something you had no clue even offended them. Be open to differences. Be willing to compromise. Be willing to let go if the demands are unbearable.

You must be aware that there are different expectations for different levels of a relationship. There are three stages to a relationship: (1) dating, (2) engaged and (3) married. You can't expect the same from all three. Stop expecting that you should get marriage benefits with a boyfriend/girlfriend title. If a person is not willing to respect your boundaries then you will find out during the initial conversation If they do not respect your boundaries, requests or desires we suggest that you cut ties with this person immediately. .

Misunderstood Silence

When you are in the dating stage and looking to get serious focus on your expectations for the future. Your topics should include; marriage, kids, financial stability, short-term goals, long-term goals, upbringing, and past relationships. Focus on what it is that they want for their life and see if it lines up with what you desire. Look to see where there can be compromises. Determine whether or not it is something that you are built for or willing to accept. Never be ashamed to discuss your past mistakes, downfalls, failures, relationships, successes, the good, bad and ugly; it is what made you who you are today. People often say to leave the past in the past, but that is one of the worst decisions that you could possibly make. You must have an understanding of where and what that person has come from in order to a.) Appreciate where they are now and b.) To gain an understanding of why they are the way they are; or why they do things the way they choose to do it. There is always a why behind the what. Keep that in mind in every relationship encounter. Hidden pasts always comes back to haunt you in the end. It is vital that the past is dealt with so that there aren't any surprises later on down the road.

Our marriage suffered greatly because there was no clear understanding of both of our pasts. We both came from two totally different backgrounds and were not exposed to the same things in life. When you have a husband whose family was deeply rooted in the church and both parents were present in their upbringing and a wife who was fatherless and was not taught the essentials of truly being a woman you are bound to have tremendous issues in your marriage if certain matters are not discussed.. Unlike my husband, I was damaged beyond measure, and he could not fathom the turmoil that brewed beneath the smile. We suffered heavily because we failed to communicate and share in detail our expectations. Your expectations are a direct reflection of who you are, and who you are is a direct reflection of where you've been.

The second stage is being engaged. By this time your focus should be on what you expect from the marriage. You should discuss roles in the household, living arrangements, finances, long term goals, how will the children be raised, what church will you attend and marital practices? This is where you get down to the "nitty gritty" of the relationship. Your focal point at this stage should be centered around how your household would be ran. Asking questions such as, *"Who will be responsible for what tasks? Will you have children? Will you have more children if one of you already has children? What will the discipline structure be? "* You may say it is not important now, but we promise it will save you from a world of chaos. It is extremely different from being in separate households to joining households. Benjamin Franklin once stated, *"If you fail to plan, then you plan to fail."* If you fail to have this conversation you are surely walking into your marriage blindfolded which we do not recommend. There will already be stress on the both of you from trying to co-habitat with one another. Don't pile on the unnecessary stress by not having a plan established.

Misunderstood Silence

Marriage is a different ball game from the first two stages. The person you married is not the same person *mentally* that you first started dating all that time ago. Richard Needham quoted *"You don't marry one person; you marry three: the person you think they are, the person they are, and the person they are going to become as the result of being."* This quote rings so true in a marriage. It is vital that you have a regular reoccurring discussions centered around your expectations. Your expectations will change just as much as you as a person will change or evolve rather. Complacency will take form if this is not being discussed, and once again we find ourselves upset at the other person for not changing with us. Have those conversations about sex, submission, likes, dislikes, performance and consistency. Be open and honest with your partner about sex. Are you enjoying the sex? Is there anything that they need to work on? Is there anything that you would like to try out. At this point you shouldn't be afraid to discuss anything. No topic should be untouchable.

You have to step out of your comfort zones and be willing to open up and be vulnerable with one another. One thing we found tremendously helpful with our marriage was having a monthly discussion. During this time we would discuss how the past month had gone in our relationship. We identified what was good and what was bad, and developed ways to improve them *together*. Think of what you or your partner can improve on. Discuss what new things you would like to implement. Be open to change and criticism. Know and understand that your partner is not trying to tear you down. They are simply trying to help you understand what it is that they need and desire from you. Don't be quick to catch an attitude or point the finger blaming them for whatever may be wrong in your relationship. Believe it or not it takes two people to make a relationship go bad. No matter what both parties could have done more or responded differently; etc. . One thing to keep in mind, is that we are all human, and we all could use improvement. Be willing to be real with one another. Nothing gets better by pretending that there isn't an issue. All you have to do is open up and say how you are *really* feeling, and also be willing to hear critique. If you feel as if the task is not easy with just the two of you look for a mediator. Find someone who will be unbiased and will not take sides. When our marriage hit rock bottom we reached out to our apostle. He pointed out both of our mistakes, and where we could implement changes. There is nothing wrong with asking for help. Sometimes you just need someone who can understand what you are saying and better communicate it with your partner.

As men we are fixers. We want to be superman and solve all of the problems. It's hard to go to another person and tell them that you need help as a man, because in the back of our mind it seems as if we've already failed. As a man you have to put your pride aside when it comes to your marriage. Truth is we don't have all the answers so it's okay to seek counsel. I do advise that you be careful of who you seek advice from, because everyone can't give unbiased and helpful counsel. There are people you just can't divulge your marital problems to or everyone and their mama will know your business. Real men know that it doesn't make you less of a man to ask for help.

Have you ever tried to tell your partner about something that offended you, and they replied by pointing out something you did as well? We have been there ourselves and sometimes still find ourselves doing it even now. Understand that everything won't be smoothed out by the morning for it takes patience and consistency. If you are willing to do the work hang in there! Know that your expectations may not be the same and that is okay. The problem comes in when you want two completely different end results. For instance he doesn't want more children because he already has two, and she has yet become a mother and wants kids of her own. Those are some things that can't be compromised.

Often times when we really want someone we tend to restructure our life to fit their wants and needs. This is never okay to do. You will wake up five years from now realizing this was never what you really wanted out of life. Sometimes your expectations will be so far apart that there is no compromising and that too is okay. Know what you really want and be true to who you are. You can only pretend for so long. Life is too short to be wasting time trying to convince yourself of something that you will never truly want or desire.

Know that there is someone out there for you. The relationship you're in now may not be the one, and that is okay. Even if your current situation doesn't work for you, know that these same guidelines can be applied to the next relationship.

Take the time to really figure out what your expectations are. What are the qualities you want your mate to possess? You must know yourself before you can help someone else understand who you are.

CHAPTER 3:
It Happened, Now What?

Often times we allow the past to dictate our future. The same goes for our relationships as well. You may often hear people say that the past is not important. But the past is very much important! Your past is the foundation to who you are, how you act and how you think. We often try to run from it, but you can't escape the past. You must face it head on. If you think it won't be a problem you are sadly mistaken. The past will eventually raise its head and become a problem. You can't deny the fact that you were hurt, offended, abused and misused.

People sometimes don't even realize they are running from the past. In our case, the past had such a strong hold on us. We both had built walls around ourselves to protect us individually. Not realizing it was doing more damage than good for our relationship. . Our past for the most part had our trust in a chokehold. We both had tremendous trust issues for different reasons. Here you have a man who doesn't trust women due to past relationships, and you have a woman who doesn't trust because she's felt abandoned all of her life. Neither one of us realized this would affect our current relationship. We pretended as if there was not an issue, and we danced around it. All we really did was create a ticking time bomb that was sure to explode, and trust it blew right up in our faces.

29

We were never truly on the same page with one another. No amount of hugs, kisses or presents could change the fact that we didn't really know each other. We didn't have a clear understanding of who we were ourselves. It took us confronting our pasts head on to be able to help each other understand what made us tick as individuals. You too must confront where you've come from and what you've been through before you can ever move forward. Not only for your relationship, but also most importantly for yourself. Once you deal with your issues you have to communicate that to your partner. One example from our relationship is that I was sensitive to the topic of rape and molestation. Then you have a husband who can't really relate, because he has never been in that situation so everything he says is wrong. For example being a woman who has dealt with molestation, and your husband has not had to deal with that type of situation. When discussing those situations he would not understand why I reacted the way I did, or why others react the way they do. He would say things like if it was me I would have said this or done that. He would not realize that those are words that could indeed rub a victim the wrong way. It would make me feel as if I brought the situation on myself. It seemed as if he was not sensitive to my situation.

We both had to compromise in that situation. He had to take the time to really understand why I felt the way that I did. I had to realize that I couldn't blame him for not having a clear understanding of something he has never been through. We had to realize that it was time for us to sit down and talk about the past. Our relationship was being attacked at so many different angles which all led back to our past. So if you think for one second that you don't have to deal with the past you might want to think twice.

You must deal with the fact that people hurt you, abandoned you, lied to you, abused you, belittled you and any other harmful thing that they might have done. You must confront the tragedies that have occurred in your life. Take the necessary time to deal with what is hurting you. You may smile, laugh and pretend as if everything is okay, but eventually it will be an issue. It will affect everything you involve yourself in. Don't allow it to run and ruin your life. It will have the ability to affect more than just relationships if you don't confront it.

We use several different ways to communicate our past. Whether it is talking to someone or writing about it. You have to find an outlet to get it out. When you're in a relationship you must have this conversation with one another. This is the moment to be completely honest and vulnerable with each other. Give them the opportunity to help you get past your issues. You're obviously in a relationship with them for a reason. Allow them to be your support system. Set a day aside to sit down and have a serious discussion on what you've been through. You have to help them understand your past. Having this conversation with your partner will help them to deal with future situations concerning you. It will allow them to be sensitive to certain subjects, and give them an understanding of how to comfort you.

If you still don't believe that your past can affect your relationship we will give you some things to think on. Do you have trust issues? Do you need more attention than the average person? Do you feel abandoned when you're alone? Do you associate a lot of things to the fact that you are fatherless/motherless? Do you tend to shy away from your true feelings? If you answered yes to any of these I can guarantee you that something in your past made you this way. Sit down and talk to your partner. If you cry every time your partner mentions getting a dog because a car hit Lassie when you were younger it's time to talk. If you get angry at your partner over the cologne or perfume they wear because your ex wore the same brand and they cheated on you with your best friend it's time to have a talk. It's time to stop displacing your feelings on your partner because of something that happened in the past. It is not fair to them.

We were recently asked to help a woman with an issue she was having with men. She couldn't figure out why she kept having trouble within her relationships. To make a long story short she couldn't trust men to be there for her because her father was so in and out of her life. The moment a relationship would get too serious she'd back away and say she only wanted to be friends.

We're here to tell you that you're going to miss out on something good because of something you can't go back and change. A lot of times we place our hurt on people who only want to be there for us. We waste our lives hoping that the offender will one day accept responsibility and apologize for their wrong doings. Truth is you may never get that apology you are looking for. Are you really going to wait? Is that one apology worth you *not* having a happy life?

You can't force anyone to accept responsibility for anything especially when they choose not to face it. You also can't force someone to apologize when they feel as if they did nothing wrong. Confront them and say what you need to say. Don't worry about if they will accept what you have to say. If you can't confront them face-to-face we strongly suggest writing it in a letter. Whatever it is that you need to do to overcome, do it!

Don't get so caught up in what the other person should do that you forget what it is you need to do. Forgive them even if they can't hear you words. Forgive them even if you never hear them apologize. You have to let it go no matter the outcome. The longer you harbor it the greater effect it will have on your relationships. This goes for both men and women.

You have to realize that you can't change the past, but you can change how it affects your life by monitoring your response to it. Take back the reigns over your life, and stop letting the past be a driving force that hinders you. The more you dwell on it the more life you give to it. It's time to wake up and overcome the past! Stop allowing it to make all of the decisions for you. It's time to put the crutches down and stand on your own two feet. A lot of times we use the past as an excuse to not allow people into our lives. We are here to tell you that it is a miserable life to live that way.

CHAPTER 4
No "I" In Team

Why is it important for each individual in a relationship to have their own dreams and goals in life? You can say that is gives you purpose. It is what helps you to remain an individual. Some may even argue that it will allow you to not get too lost into the other person. It may even allow you to not be so dependent on a person and give you something to do. There is nothing wrong with that. We encourage people to have dreams. Chase after them with everything that's within you.. You must do what makes you happy.

Discuss your dreams and goals before you even commit to the commitment of a relationship. You need to know if you two are on the same highway going in the same direction. You don't have to have the same dreams, but you do need to be able to compliment one another. If her dream is to be on the front page of King Magazine so she starts stripping to make connections it won't work out if your goal is to run for Mayor. Don't wait until you've fallen deeply for one another to realize that you two want totally different lifestyles.

So what do you do when what you want from your relationship does not align with your personal goals? Take us for an example: I have always been interested in modeling. I am beautiful and photographers want to work with me. Then you have my husband who is not comfortable with certain attire, and he doesn't understand where the art comes into play with the photo session. The only thing he can see is that I am half naked. For a while I compromised and only did photos that he approved of. Eventually I stopped altogether because I realized that I would have to choose. It was either have creative freedom to do the shoots the way I wanted or quit all together. You may say, *"Well, that was her fault to give up on her dreams!"* No, I realized that my relationship meant more than the photos did.

Every dream and goal that you have will not always align with your relationship. With dreams come sacrifices, and the same goes for your relationship. There will come a time when you must decide what is more important. When we were engaged to be married, we had to sit down and align our goals to get on the same page or we would be setting ourselves up for failure. Everyone has dreams and ambitions. It's not the dream that is the problem perhaps it may be how you pursue it.

When you are just dating you don't have as many responsibilities to that person versus if you were married. More than likely you were already chasing your dream before that person came into the picture. Regardless of what title is on the relationship there are things you have to consider. Are you neglecting your partner for your dream? Are you not showing enough attention to them? Are you barely listening when they are speaking? Has it been a minute since your last date because you are always working? Does your goals and desires align? The list goes on. If you see a serious future with this person or you are married then you have to consider them when you are making your plans for the future.

You can have these grand dreams, but do these dreams include the person you're with? Is this dream just for you or for the both of you? You must communicate your goals to one another. Determine whether or not that is something your partner is willing to support. What are some things that can be compromised on? Include yourself into their dreams and they should do the same. You have to be their biggest cheerleader. Set goals for where you are trying to get as a *team.* Your significant other can be the best support person for you.

Every relationship is a team. You cannot make any decisions without thinking, *'how is this going to affect my significant other?'* There is no way to make those types of decisions without them. So when you are in a relationship and you have new goals you have to ask yourself how would my husband or wife feel about this? Do you feel like it would be a problem? If so, either you should consider amending your goals or altering them in some shape or form. I'm not saying give up on your dreams but you should be considerate of your significant other when you are making your goals. Believe me it's lonely at the top so having someone to share it with is so much sweeter.

Another scenario to deal with is the couple that has the same dreams or who is building an empire together. One thing you have to be careful when going after the same thing is the potential of jealousy. If you reach the dream first will your partner be genuinely happy for your success or will it cause a rift in the relationship. If you're building a business or ministry together don't get so caught up in the job that you lose focus on each other. Make time to go out on a date, cuddle up on the sofa to watch a movie, go bowling, or take a vacation. Whatever you do don't forget about each other's needs. Make time to nurture your relationship.

The two of you need to be on the same page. This will give you the opportunity to grow together. There is nothing like having someone there every step of the way to help push you to that next level.

No dream is too big or too small. Something that we found very helpful was focusing on one milestone at a time. Working on multiple things at once can be counterproductive. Working on multiple things will only cause something to go unfinished and you do not want that. You don't want to wake up one day and realize you lost everything you loved because you were too busy working on your passions

Dreams change over time. You start a mission you complete it and then you go to the next. Every time you start a new tasks communicate that with your significant other. You always want to keep an open line of communication. Effective communication
takes consistency even if it's a planned event with your significant other. Take the time out to have those conversations. It will bless you in the long run.

We've all heard the old saying, *"There's no "I" in team,"* and that's exactly how you have to look at it. It doesn't matter if you were working on these dreams before they came along. They are here now, and you have to revise your plans. Ask yourself is this the person who you plan to have by your side? If not, why are you even in a relationship with them to begin with? You have to include them into the grand scheme of things.

You must consider whether or not this person is worth revising your plans for. Are they going to be a good support system? So often we get caught up in the whim of what we think is love, and we don't actually consider the greater details. Have you truly considered the longevity of this person in your life? We are not advising you to break up, but we do want you to sit down and really think of all the pros and cons and review your relationship objectively.

Our goal is to help you avoid the situation of waking up one day and realizing you gave up on all your hopes and dreams. We do not want you to regret your mate in the long run. This is why having these type of conversations are important.

CHAPTER 5
Let's Talk Money

Truth is money does not buy happiness but it does cut down on a lot of confusion. When it comes to finances in a relationship you have to know your role. Lack of financial planning only causes additional stress and unwanted burdens on your relationship. Whether it is due to over spending or bad credit. It may not seem like a problem now but when the bills start piling up and you see no way out it can take a toll on your relationship. A lot of people live above their means in an effort to keep up with the next person. If you can't afford it, don't spend it. You are only setting yourself back.

Ask yourself, "When have I written out a monthly budget?" When was the last time you had to borrow money? Why did you have to borrow money? What's the first thing you did the last time you got paid? Do you write out a list when you shop for groceries? How many online purchases do you make a month? What is your credit score? How many bills are you late on? How many loans are in your name? The list goes on and on.

It all leads back to frivolous spending which occurs when you are constantly shopping and not watching what goes in and what comes out. You have to manage your funds closely. When you are in a marriage or relationship it is vital that you be disciplined and monitor your finances. What happens when you don't have money for food or your rent because you have spent all of your money? What do you say to your significant other when you don't have the rent money or the light bill? You have to be mindful and considerate of your other priorities. Stop buying Starbucks everyday if you are already behind on your rent. Don't buy those new pair of red bottoms or those new pair of Jordan's if you can barely put gas in your car.

You have to make smarter choices with your money. Whenever you marry someone you also marry their debt. Know what you are getting yourself into. Ask questions, and ask a lot of them. There's nothing wrong with asking a person what their credit score is. In this day and age it is hard to purchase anything without a decent credit history. The way a person spends will tell you a lot about who they are. You can't be afraid to have this conversation.

Money is a taboo conversation in a lot of households due to a failure to have effective communication established. A lack of finances causes a ripple effect of stressors. When was the last time you sat down with your partner to discuss a budget for the month? If you haven't had this conversation it needs to happen today. You should know what is coming in and most importantly what is going out.

Money management is the key. Though it is important to know your partner's credit score, it is equally important to know your own. Is it good or bad? If it is the latter, then what are you doing to fix it? Here are a few suggestions:

- Create a monthly budget.
- Write down your expenses.

- Determine what's left over.
- Set aside money for your savings.
- Stick to the budget!

Expenses can include anything from you tithes and offering to your light bill. We suggest you create your budget the moment you know what your paycheck is going to be. Make sure that you also put money away into your savings account. If you didn't put it in the budget then don't spend it especially if you're living paycheck to paycheck. One of the worse things you can do is go out and get a loan only to add to your long list of bills.

So you've created a budget now what? You can't forget to run your budget by your partner. Now if you aren't married you can't expect someone to be this open as if you were, but if you are i married this is a step you cannot skip. Discuss what bills need to be paid, and who's going to pay what bills. This goes hand in hand with knowing what is expected. If you know you're not going to have enough money to pay every bill determine which are the most important. If you need to disconnect services then do so. It's not necessary that you have a cell phone and house phone. It's not necessary to pay for Wi-Fi when there are libraries; etc. It's not necessary to pay for cable when you can watch videos and movies on Netflix or Hulu; or even dvds. Sometimes you have to make sacrifices. You can't always have it all especially when you dreams, goals and visions in which you desire to see manifested in your life. Until you get to where you desire to be you may have to give up a few things until you get to a place where you have a savings account, your bills are being paid on time and you are following your monthly budget. Another option you have in saving tremendously especially when it comes to household supplies and groceries is learning how to coupon. This has become very popular over the years and it really works. Y

There are so many options to choose from when you are trying to save money. If it takes you pinching pennies for the next six months then do what you have to do. You have to get to a place where enough is enough. If one of you are spending more than you are depositing then it should be addressed immediately. Stop being afraid to speak up because you don't want to make the other person mad or you're afraid they may threaten to leave you. Sometimes you just have to take that risk, because eventually you both will be broke and busted.

Financial stability takes a great deal of consistency. You can't save and do a budget for two paychecks and think you have fixed the issue. Financial stability takes commitment. You have to be dedicated to enforcing a routine and sticking to it. The moment you slip you will find yourself in the same predicament as before or even worse. Budgeting is not an option. You need your significant other there to keep you disciplined and vice versa. Hold them accountable for their actions. Stop enabling them to continue on with bad habits.

You'll never be able to take that vacation, buy your dream home, get that new car, or save for a rainy day if you don't get your finances in order now. The strain that is being caused on your relationship will either get better or worse but the decision is yours.

Along your journey to financial freedom it's important to be able to distinguish between y needs and wants. Everyone's basic needs are food, shelter, and clothing. That's all you need to survive on a day-to-day basis. You don't need that loose wave Brazilian hair, a new watch, three new dresses, a pair of Raybans or an iPhone 6. You need to save. It's not an option, because things pop up. Don't be the one to say, "I wish I hadn't spent that $250 now that I need a new tire." You must learn to save for that rainy day, because it will come.

We can remember a time when we hit a pothole, and ended up spending over a thousand dollars on a tire, rim, lug nuts and all kinds of stuff. The mechanic shop refused to deal with our insurance company. We ended having to pay for the full amount, and then wait to be reimbursed only half of it by our insurance company. What if we didn't have the money? We needed our car for work. Our schedules didn't align for us to only have access to one car. Not being able to pay for it could have had a ton of negative effects. You must be prepared for the things you didn't budget for as well.

We've witnessed so many couples drown in debt to the point that it ruined their relationship. There's the couple where one is trying to buy love that can't be bought so the bills continuously pile up. There's the couple that's trying to keep up with the other couples around them. If you have to pay to make them stay, then it's time to release them.

We all believe in unconditional love. There is nothing unconditional about being in debt just to satisfy your significant other. They should be there to add substance to your life not take away from. Know your finances, know your limits and stick to it.

CHAPTER 6
Beware of Outsiders

Before you got into this relationship you already had your own set of family and friends. They were the people in which you received the most of your solicited advice from. They are usually the ones you approach to ask if a person fits you or is good enough for you. You take their advice whether or not they give good advice simply because they seem to know you the best. This is a common trend amongst new relationships. We all do this in some shape or form.

Most people introduce that someone special to their friends first. It's been proven that if you can make it through a person's friends then you will more than likely meet their family as well. You look for that stamp of approval. It usually starts off on a good foot until things get serious, but sometimes it then becomes an issue.

When things become serious the complaints start. You're spending too much time together. You're not the same anymore. They're changing you for the worst. You traded us for your new boo. We barely see you anymore. Friends tend to feel abandoned especially when they are single and you find someone. What do you do at this point?

How do you address these situations? Do you tell your significant other how your friends feel about them? Do you choose between your significant other and friends? Do you put your friends in their place? When will you have enough? Where do you draw the line?

The worst thing you can do is hearing your friends disrespect your significant other and say absolutely nothing. You are giving them permission to be disrespectful if you do not address it. To make matters even worse will be if you don't tell your significant other what is being said. You owe them that right if this is the relationship you are going to be in. Don't allow them to think that everything is peaches and cream when there are malicious words being said behind their backs. What happens if they walk in on a bashing conversation about them and you haven't enlightened them on what has been said? That's an offense that is hard to take back. They will base future situations off of that one event.

Some of the same things happen with your families. Families can be a lot more judgmental of your relationship. They feel as if they know what you need better than anyone. Many problems can arrive from that. What happens when no one is good enough for you? How do you address your family? It's a lot harder to disappoint family rather than friends. Sometimes we feel obligated to make our family happy especially your immediate family members.

The most common relationship agitator from families is usually the mother. Take our marriage for instance. You have a man who is the baby of a family where only boys were born. The mother was used to a date every week, a shopping partner, someone to keep her company and to top it off he was the last one to leave the nest. The relationship was very close nit so her approval was crucial to the relationship. Due to this relationship there were times were boundaries were crossed.

One of the hardest relationships is between mother in-laws and daughter in-laws. This was our situation. What do you do when your mother crosses the line and your significant other hears what is said? Do you disappoint your mother by standing up for them, or do you give her a pass because of who she is? In our case it was necessary that the situation be dealt with instantly. The mother didn't have to be disrespected in order for it to be addressed. It's not about what you do but how you do it.

When dealing with a situation similar to this the first thing you should do is put a stop to it. Whoever the offender is should be confronted at that moment. Depending on your relationship with that person will determine what you say and how you say it. Apologize to your significant other especially if they did nothing to warrant the insult. Remember if you don't stand up for them then who will. Do not allow it to build up to the point where they have to stand up for themselves and there's a major blow up. You wouldn't want anyone disrespecting you from their side so don't allow it from yours.

Family and friends aren't the only outside relationships you have to deal with. You also have co-workers and social media friends. How do these people play a role in your relationship? More frequently these relationships are becoming a bigger issue.

One reason is because people are being more open about their relationships with those who shouldn't be included.

We develop a great deal of associates at work. We go out to lunch together. We sit around and talk about what's going on in our lives. You have no idea who else these people are spreading your business too. You must be careful in the information you give out about your relationship. The worst feeling is telling all your business then having your significant other come up to your job to visit and everyone is staring at them with the side eye. They can feel as if something is wrong, but no one will say what it is. Then they are left wondering what did they do, and why is everyone staring at them.

There was a situation where a woman was talking about how she and her husband were trying to have a baby. She knew she was very fertile due to the six kids she already had, but they hadn't gotten pregnant yet. She then revealed that it was due to him giving her a STD. She thought that she was whispering, but everyone could hear her conversation. Her husband eventually visited and everyone was looking at him with the side eyes, and you could tell he was uncomfortable. You have to learn that there is a time and place for everything.

You also have that one bitter co-worker who is the "Negative Nancy" of relationships. They are always giving out reasons of why you shouldn't be in a relationship. Every time you bring up an argument that you and your significant other had they tell you to pack up and leave. Beware of these people the more you hang around them, the more they'll convince you to leave. Remember misery loves company. You'll end up just as bitter and lonely as they are.

Social media has become a burden for a lot of relationships. You can connect with millions of people around the world. Though social media can be good in so many ways, you know there has to be some bad that comes with it as well. People are calling social media a relationship killer. Truth is social media isn't killing relationships, people are. There have to be boundaries set in place. Using social media goes hand in hand with expectations. How do you expect your significant other to behave on social media?

In order to set boundaries it has to be discussed. Will your relationship status be public? Will you have a joint account? What types of pictures are allowed to be posted? What content is deemed inappropriate to share? What will you do when you get inappropriate messages? Will you show your significant other? You have to be on the same page. You don't want any surprises.

It is so easy to screenshot and forward messages. You never know if someone is trying to set you up so that they can put you on blast. Just because it is not inappropriate to you doesn't mean your significant other will take it the same way. You have to be sensitive to what makes them uncomfortable. Also think about if it will upset you, more than likely it will upset them as well. Remember what's good for the goose is good for the gander. Don't be a hypocrite.

Somewhere a line has to be drawn in all of these situations. The problem is determining when and where will it happen? We suggest the sooner the better. If you deal with it as soon as the problem arrive you won't deal with it for long. If you constantly allow the disrespect to happen the harder it will be to get people to take the relationship serious. It starts with the first incident, and how you react to it. Whether it be confronting a family member, friend or your significant other. You must correct the offender immediately. You never want to get to a point where someone asks you to choose one over the other.

CHAPTER 7
The "S" Word

The most common and uncomfortable subject to approach is sex. When is the last time you discussed your sex life with your significant other? Openly talking about sex with your partner has become such a taboo topic as well. People avoid this topic like the plague, and pretend it doesn't exist. Couples are simply doing the do without doing their homework.

It is common to use previous sex practices in new relationships. You figure that if it works for one then it works for all right? Wrong! Just because Diane liked it this way doesn't mean Trina will enjoy the same antics and vice versa. You must ask questions when it comes to your sex life.

Are you satisfied with the physicality of your relationship? If not, have you discussed it with your partner? If you haven't had this conversation ask yourself why not? Are you afraid of the subject? Do you not want to deal with the backlash? Will your partner have an instant attitude? What do you do when your physical needs aren't being met? Eventually it will take a toll on your relationship, and have you doing things outside of your character.

Do you know if your partner is happy with your sex life? How are you so sure? Have you asked? Do you know their likes and dislikes? You must do your homework on what it is that turns them on. How can you expect to really please them if you haven't asked any of these questions? There may even be things from their past holding them back.

In our case you I was sexually abused as a child and certain actions would take me back to that situation. I can remember being a little girl and at the time we lived in a four-bedroom house with all of our cousins, aunts, uncles and grandmother, and all the children slept on the floor on a pallet together. One of my older male cousins molested me. It would have been considered rape had he realized that he never penetrated me. I was holding my thighs together so tightly that he assumed he was inside of me since we were in the dark. I can remember crying and shaking and just waiting for it to be over because it wasn't the first time. I felt so dirty and humiliated after he ejaculated between my thighs. I can still remember what his semen felt like. Till this day I freak out with my own husband if his seeds spill on me, and I'm his wife.

We also had that relationship that just assumed we knew what another liked. For a long time we were in the dark, because we really had no clue on how to please one another. We failed to communicate our wants and needs to each other. This is a mistake a lot of couples often make.

Neither of us were really happy sexually, but we were married so we were content. We were no longer the same individuals we were when we first met. Our sex life had changed drastically. We went from ripping each other's clothes off every time we saw one another to maybe being involved sexually twice a week if we were lucky. The million dollar question people want to know is if sex changes after marriage, and the answer is yes. It is up to the two you if it gets better or worse.

It's easy to allow the flame to dwindle in the bedroom. You get complacent with a routine. You allow work and kids to consume you, and you forget to please one another sexually. Here are some suggestions to keep it sexy:

- Send naughty texts throughout the day to build anticipation.
- Send teasing photos.
- Send the kids to grandma's house for the weekend.
- Go on a random getaway it doesn't have to be far.
- Light some candles, run a nice warm bath for two, get some rose petals, turn on some slow jams and set the mood.
- Keeping it sexy doesn't always have to include sex: massages, candle lit dinners, a night of slow dancing and etc.

We never like to point fingers and blame one person for a lack thereof, because in some shape or form we both played a part no matter how small it was. You have a husband that didn't do study the woman he married to know that her past would eventually affect their sex life. You have a wife who has always used sex to keep people in her life so the moment she finds something real she figures she no longer has to do the same things. This is why we stated that you must talk about the past and what happened prior to you two uniting with one another.

Though we knew of the past we never connected the two together.

I was abandoned by her father, didn't have a close relationship with her mother growing up and she envied her siblings for their fathers. I couldn't figure out why people didn't want to be a real part of her life. Only to discover that men were drawn to my chocolate skin, and that I could use my body to make them stay around at least for a little while until I found someone else. Then when I found the one God had made just for me I treated him like everyone else. That's what our marriage was based off of. That's what happens when you don't confront the past and deal with it.

Then you have a husband who is from a completely different world, and doesn't understand the type of life his wife once lived nor experienced. I assumed that because I already had sex prior to her that I knows exactly what she likes. Only to wake up 3 years into the relationship and find out that I'm not pleasing my wife as well as I assumed. Nothing hurts a man's pride more than to know that he may not be satisfying his wife sexually. Things that are common and turns most people on failed to do so for my wife. I had to decide whether to take that on as a challenge or accept defeat. This made us realize that you have to do more than just listen when a person tells you about their past. You have to make sure you really get a clear understanding of what you're walking into, and that is done by asking questions.

Misunderstood Silence

You need to know how things in the past affected them mentally. Know that every man and woman are not the same. It may take a different approach to reach the same result. Do not box yourself in and have a closed mind to think that your way is the best way. That will drive a person to two results: leaving or cheating. There must be a reoccurring conversation about your sex life with your partner. You must be open to hear the truth from them as well Don't get upset if they tell you that you're lacking in a certain area. Be honored that instead of stepping outside of your relationship they came to you so that the two of you can figure it out together.

One thing we like to do is sit down once a month and go over our relationship. We discuss both the good and bad. You can't just only talk about the good or only the bad. There has to a balance. If all you do is refer to the good then you're living in a fantasyland pretend everything is perfect when there is always something to work on and improve. If you are only approaching the bad then eventually you will feel attacked, and think that nothing you do is good enough. You must create a healthy balance.

Really be willing to listen, and know that the conversation is not to tear you down. It is to strengthen your relationship as a whole. Learn to stop taking everything so personal, and be willing to make the situation better. Would you rather your significant other tell you exactly how they are feeling or would you like for them to go find comfort elsewhere? You must be approachable in any relationship. No one wants to talk to a person who is always biting their heads off if they have an issue.

There's an old cliché that says, *"What you won't do another one will."* There is never a good enough excuse for cheating on your partner, but you must be realistic. For every action there is a cause. Everything you do has a reason. You go to work to pay bills. You work out to lose weight. You take medicine to get better. So what makes you think that people don't have a reason for cheating? No one cheats just because for no reason. You don't wake up and decide that today is the day you will cheat. Something brought you to this point.

If your significant other cheats and you decide to stay, be willing to ask the hard questions. Know that you may not like the answer. The process of restoring your relationship is not going to be easy. You may dream about the situation. You may even think of it out of the blue. The best thing you can do is talk about it. Don't allow it to eat you alive and consume your relationship. If you said that you are going to forgive then you can't use it as ammo for future arguments.

It was so hard for our marriage at first. It played on our emotions and took us on a rollercoaster ride. There were plenty of times we both thought it would be better to just split. We were young with no kids so it would be easy to start over. If we would have walked away we wouldn't be able to help you fix your situation.

We could have avoided this entire scenario if we had only sat down and really communicated all of these things ahead of time.

Misunderstood Silence

We were going off of assumptions pretending that everything was okay in our marriage when it really wasn't. It had gotten to the point where our pretending even fooled us.

All it takes for you to open up your mouth and say something. Say what you want, and say what you need. If you are offended say something the moment it happens. Don't wait to bring it up in the middle of a disagreement that is about something totally different. If your partner is coming to you with a concern don't brush it aside just because you don't agree with them. They aren't going to feel the exact same as you. Treat their concerns just as serious as you would yours.

You must remember that your spouse has physical needs. Your job is to fulfill those needs. Learn what pleases and excites them. Make the journey to finding what they like joyful. Then again they may like some things that may be totally off limits to you. You won't know these things unless you both sit down and talk about it. Open up! Speak up! Confront the unknown. Remember misunderstood silence is the worst kind of them all.

CHAPTER 8
You Live & You Learn

We can almost guarantee that every couple reading this book can attest that they have dealt with at least one of these issues. Like we've stated before you are not alone. We have dealt with each and every one of these issues in our own marriage. By no means are we claiming that we know all the answers and rules to relationships. We are simply providing you with insight from a marriage that was one step away from being divorced. Our goal is to teach others how to avoid what we went through.

True enough every relationship is different, but the groundwork is all the same. Every issue that you may face inside of your relationship requires one simple thing "effective communication." As simple as it seems, it is the hardest thing to do. We get so caught up in what we need and want that we forget the needs of others. You can't be selfish in a relationship.

You must remember that your thoughts are not their thoughts, and your reactions are not their reactions. A lot of times we find ourselves upset with our partners because they didn't react the way we expected them to. Truth is we are really upset because they didn't react the way we would have. You must remember that just because it's a serious matter to you doesn't mean that they may feel the same way. There will be times where you may feel as if something is pointless and they feel like it is a matter of life or death. Feeling this way is normal but this is also the time when you must step outside of yourself.

It's not going to always be about what you feel is right or wrong. Relationships take a great deal of compromise and respecting the views of the one you love. In order to have a successful and healthy relationship you both must e willing to confront your issues head on and love one another past each of them. There is nothing worse than sweeping the problems under the rug and pretending as if they do not exist.. It's like a ticking time bomb just waiting to explode. Be willing to really listen to what your partner is saying to you.

There are many times where our loved ones come to us just to say how they are really feeling about the relationship. Often times we instantly jump to defense mode ready to put up a fight. Know that they aren't there to tear you down or hurt your feelings. They are simply there to express a need that is simply not being met. If you are the one needing to express an issue then you also have to be careful. Be mindful of your approach and tone. You never want to make your partner feel attacked.

One thing we like to do is give a positive for every negative which leads to a healthy balance. If you only talk when there is an issue then they will feel as if nothing they do is right. Be willing to compliment and commend them on a job well done. A little goes a long way in relationships. Learn to care for the needs of the other person as well as your own.

We understand that there will be times when you will need to be alone to think things through. Know that time apart won't fix the issue neither will pretending that nothing is wrong. We had a woman say that she was going to get her hair cut and colored to make her feel better. She then came back to say that her husband had been laying the compliments on thick! The one thing she never said is that they talked about their issues and came up with a solution. After all was said and done she was still dealing with the chaos inside her marriage. You can't buy a new wardrobe to dress up (or cover up) the issues you are having in your relationship Once a month we sit down and discuss our marriage. We talk about what is going well, and what needs some work. We leave our emotions out of the conversation which has helped us tremendously.

You both are two people who will continuously grow as time goes on. It is vital that you have these conversations. You will grow to want new things as you evolve as a person. These conversations have to be reoccurring ones. We titled this book *Misunderstood Silence* for a reason. When you don't communicate with your partner the only choice they have is to assume that what they are doing is right. You cannot be upset with them for something they didn't know. Don't assume that they should know what it is that you want or desire as it relates to any part of your marriage.

It won't get better over night, but if you remain consistent you can definitely change the situation around. This book may even help you figure out that the current relationship you are in may not be the one for you. But you will never know until you talk about it. So open up, be vulnerable, ask questions, talk, listen, understand, compromise and be patient. What's meant to be will be for love never fails.

"Without continual growth and progress, such words as improvement, achievement, and success have no meaning." – Benjamin Franklin

Jeffrey and Chanel Nash

ABOUT THE AUTHOR

Chanel and Jeffrey Nash are newly published authors who are here to educate, motivate and inspire the masses. After completely restoring their marriage they set out on a journey to help others restore their lives and relationships. They are the CEO and founders of The Nash Restoration Project, where they teach others how to admit to their problems, confront their issues and restore their lives by allowing God to be in control of their situation and guide their footsteps.

www.thenashrestorationproject.com

Jeffrey and Chanel Nash

Jeffrey and Chanel Nash

45709029R00037